THE
7 STEPS TO
STARDOM

How to Become
a Working Actor
in Movies, TV,
and Commercials

CHRISTINA FERRA-GILMORE

Applause Theatre & Cinema Books   New York

The 7 Steps to Stardom: How to Become a Working Actor in Movies,
TV, & Commercials by Christina Ferra-Gilmore
©2006 Christina Ferra-Gilmore

The accompanying DVD is ©2006 Wink Martindale Enterprises and Christina Ferra-Gilmore.

BOOK DESIGN BY PEARL CHANG   ILLUSTRATIONS BY JUN PARK

LIBRARY OF CONGRESS CATALOGING-IN-PUBLICATION DATA

Ferra-Gilmore, Christina.
    The 7 steps to stardom : how to become a working actor in movies, tv, & commercials / by Christina Ferra-Gilmore.
    p.   cm.
ISBN-13: 978-1-55783-678-6
ISBN-10: 1-55783-678-7
    1. Acting—Vocational guidance. I. Title: Seven steps to stardom. II. Title.
PN2055.F47 2006
792.02'8023—dc22   2006001697

The *7 Steps to Stardom* is a trademark of Christina Ferra-Gilmore and the Actor's Edge Studio.

APPLAUSE THEATRE & CINEMA BOOKS
19 West 21st Street, Suite 201
New York, NY 10010
Phone 212.575.9265
Fax 212.575.9270
Email: info@applausepub.com
Internet: www.applausepub.com

Applause books are available through your local bookstore, or you may order at www.applausepub.com or call Music Dispatch at 800-637-2852.

SALES & DISTRIBUTION

North America:
  Hal Leonard Corp.
  7777 West Bluemound Road
  P. O. Box 13819
  Milwaukee, WI 53213
  Phone: (414) 774-3630
  Fax: (414) 774-3259
  Email: halinfo@halleonard.com
  Internet: www.halleonard.com

Europe:
  Roundhouse Publishing Ltd.
  Millstone, Limers Lane
  Northam, North Devon EX 39 2RG
  Phone: (0) 1237-474-474
  Fax: (0) 1237-474-774
  Email: roundhouse.group@ukgateway.net

This book is dedicated with greatest love and affection to my family,

Mary Lou, Tony, Sandy, Wink, and Gene.

I could not have achieved many things in life without your love and support.

And, most specially to my son, Leo.

Your love, light, and joy have graced my life with purpose.

Also, to my loving spiritual family,

Bob, Marc, Sara, Carl, Ed, Rene, Rebecca, Alan, Stephan,

Elise, Aunt Sis, Carolyn, Don, Malou, and the Marco family.

I appreciate you.

ACKNOWLEDGEMENTS

The author wishes to thank her producers,
Wink and Sandy Martindale.

Also a special thanks to Ed Lojeski.

Thanks to Michael Messina, Pearl Chang, Brian Black and everyone
at Applause, Bill Retherford, Gene Gilmore, Christopher Cvijetic,
Sheila Kay, Brian McManus, Nick Chavez of the Nick Chavez Salon,
Michael Harris, Esq., and Chuck Hurewitz, Esq.

Thank you to our dynamic industry professionals:
Alan Bailey, Bob Wall, Bill Dance of Bill Dance Casting,
Steve Stevens of The Stevens Group, Elvis Presley, Sandra Lord,
Sara Ballantine, Dr. Boris Bagdassarroff, Stephan Valero at
Print Models Network, and Walter Lawson, Esq.

Thank you to our actors: Richard Herranz, Dena Paduano,
David Dortch, Rudy Rodriguez, Jose Solano, Rember Martinez, Alan
Sanders, Jackie Warden, Mark Muranyi, Steve Peterson, Sonia
Melgar, Veronica Castro, David Weisman, Bud Tyndale, Tyson Russell,
Andrew Mullin, Jacqui Lugo, and Nathan Luginbill.

And most importantly, thank you to God for all blessings.

CONTENTS

FROM THE AUTHOR

So you want to be a working actor!

This book—and the companion DVD—will help you take control.

It doesn't matter if you're a beginner—or a professional whose career has hit a wall. This package provides you with The Seven Steps to Stardom. These are the fundamentals you need to start a career—or jumpstart one.

All Seven Steps are absolutely essential. Some deal with the artistic side of acting. Some deal with the business side. To be a successful working actor, you must be intimately familiar with both.

Let me put it this way: if you're not making progress in the industry, you've probably tripped over—or skipped over—at least one of the Seven Steps.

Of course, there's no guarantee. There's another element called "luck." But I promise you this: take the Seven Steps, and you'll be doing what virtually all professional working actors do to be successful.

Maybe you'll be like my friends Sara Ballantine or Lance Legault: busy, hard-working actors known throughout the industry, supporting their families not only with their strong acting talents but with their business savvy and total professionalism.

Or maybe you'll be the next Al Pacino, Eddie Murphy, or Julia Roberts—name actors known all over the world.

The difference between these two sets of actors has nothing to do with talent or professionalism. There's always the "luck factor." Will you get a significant role in a major picture with the production budget and power distribution to launch a superstar career? Maybe. But whatever scenario you fall in—star or working actor—if you follow the Seven Steps wisely, you'll become a highly respected, well-paid artist.

Focus all of your energy on taking the Steps—and the possibilities are endless!

I wish you the best of success! God bless!

Sincerely,

Christina Ferra-Gilmore

Actor's Edge Studio/Hollywood, California

STEP 1

YOU ARE THE PRODUCT

Be the best that you can be

The bottom line: *You* are a product.

Your first task in establishing a career: What kind of actor-product are you?

To determine that, you've got to take an honest inventory of what you've got to sell. During this evaluation process, there is no room for ego.

Meaning this: if you're thirty-five years old—don't try to play someone who's twenty. Go that route and a real twenty-year-old will beat you for the part.

Instead, compete with people in your physical age range. That way, you stand a chance of beating the competition. Makes sense, doesn't it? But it does mean putting your ego in escrow.

And defining the product means more than just playing your age range. What about your physical attributes? Your personality essence? Are you the handsome leading man? A happy-go-lucky "next-door" neighbor? A rough-looking character type who could play a drug dealer? Really, it doesn't matter. Hollywood needs them all. What type are you?

Your special skills in other areas will also help you become a money-making product in the acting industry. Can you sing? Can you dance? These skills will allow you to act in musical theatre.

Can you play a musical instrument? What if the role you are up for is the life story of a famous musician?

If you are an expert at martial arts, you might get your break acting in a movie which also requires this skill, just as Bob Wall and Chuck Norris did when they were in a Bruce Lee film.

MY PRODUCT INVENTORY

Parts I Could Play

PROJECT TITLE	MEDIA	BRIEF DESCRIPTION OF CHARACTER
(and genre)	*(TV/movie/comm)*	*(Role description/Occupation/Age range)*

More Parts I Could Play

PROJECT TITLE (and genre)	MEDIA (TV/movie/comm)	BRIEF DESCRIPTION OF CHARACTER (Role description/Occupation/Age range)

Being an expert at any sport can help your acting career, if there are acting roles which also require that skill. Look how being a successful bodybuilder helped Arnold Schwarznegger begin a successful acting career!

Therefore, take your other talents into account while taking your product inventory.

Taking a physical, emotional, spiritual and skill inventory of this unique product—you—takes four weeks.

Here's your assignment: For the next four weeks, watch all the TV, movies, commercials and plays that you possibly can. Put your ego aside, drop the fantasies—and every time you see a part that you could *realistically* play, fill in the columns on the worksheet.

By the end of four weeks, your page should be filled with a variety of roles. Then look for the common thread. It won't take long to tell if you're the comedic sidekick or the romantic lead in a soap.

But as you fill in the columns, assess yourself bluntly and dispassionately, without prejudice. If you're the chubby, funny-looking sitcom type—and there's nothing wrong with that—don't put yourself down as the boyfriend opposite Julia Roberts. Unless they're doing a remake of *10*, you won't get the part.

YOUR PHYSICALITY

I like to think of aspiring actors as uncut diamonds, all with a potential worth of millions of dollars—maybe hundreds of millions. The aspiring actor has many facets, just as a diamond does. Let's look at some of the most important facets, namely your physical facet, your mental and emotional facet, your spiritual facet, the facet of your acting skills (which we will take a look at in Step 2), and the setting that you anchor your diamond in, the financial plan. Remember that all diamonds have inclusions, or "flaws." That's okay. Let's just work on honing each facet of your diamond until you are so valuable, the inclusions don't matter.

And while I readily acknowledge that your soul is infinite and limitless, the physical body you inhabit has certain limitations. *No matter what you look like, your look will limit you in some areas and help you excel in others.* Never forget the handsome leading man may have difficulty getting a part as a tough guy.

Your job—after identifying the roles that your look allows you to play—is to take that look and exploit it. Emphasize what you've got. Develop your look to be even stronger than it already is.

If you've got the "bad guy" look, make yourself even scarier. There are lots of ways. Clothes, haircut, hair color, earring, tattoo, mustache, a heavy beard, or maybe just a five o'clock shadow: what can you do to look like a *really* bad guy?

You're a sexy romantic lead? Do things to be even more attractive than you already are. Bleach your teeth. Pump up. Slim down. Ditch the glasses and wear contacts. Cut your hair short or let it grow long. Whatever shows you at your best—develop a look that's strong, clear, identifiable—and uniquely *you* (emphasizing your strong essence).

MY PHYSICALITY WORKSHEET
A Personal Inventory

Based on my "product inventory," here's a description of the type of characters I will play:

_____

_____

_____

_____

What can I do to help me achieve that look?

_____

_____

_____

_____

_____

HAIR *(cut, style, color?)*

_____

_____

_____

_____

EYES *(contacts, glasses?)*

_____

_____

continued on next page >>

MY PHYSICALITY WORKSHEET (cont'd)
A Personal Inventory

TEETH: (whiten, straighten, bond, veneers?)

COMPLEXION: (acne, large pores, scars, wrinkles?)

BODY: (lose/gain weight, bulk up/cardio, diet?)

Mercedes-Benz didn't get to where it is today by trying to be Toyota. McDonald's never pretends to be a fancy restaurant.

But whether you're a sensitive romantic lead or the nerdy intellectual type, you must keep your body in shape. Be healthy, like an athlete training for the Olympics. Disciplined. After all, you *are* "going for the gold." So no smoking and light on the alcohol, if at all. Eat healthy every day and work out consistently. And no drugs whatsoever.

My father and mother—Tony and Mary Lou Ferra—were successful nightclub owners who hobnobbed with some of the greatest names in Hollywood. A few of them—dear friends of theirs, most in the music industry—destroyed themselves with alcohol or drugs. Either they died young or wound up a screaming headline on the front cover of a rag sheet. Addicts don't last, in show business or any other business.

Even those who survived worked only sporadically. After all, why should a producer deal with someone who's unpredictable and unprofessional when there are plenty of healthy, productive people around?

So keep your body sober and glowing with health. After all, one of the definitions of "star" is "luminous body."

YOUR MENTAL AND EMOTIONAL STATE

No matter how talented or attractive an actor is, if they have misconceptions or personality problems, i.e., the wrong mindset, they will either make their path to success much harder, or never achieve success at all! My mother (who was an actress on live television) taught me a very helpful set of words which facilitate success in any business—the "P" words.

PROFESSIONALISM

PATIENCE

PERSISTENCE

PROACTION

POWER OF POSITIVE THINKING

Now one at a time:

PROFESSIONALISM: Show business is just that, a business of writing, casting, producing, and marketing shows whether they are movies, television shows, shows which go to DVD or the Internet, industrial shows, or shows for theatre.

A casting director who hires you, and producers who ultimately pay you to act in their project, do it for one reason. Not because you're "special," and not because people in your hometown think you're cute—but because you contribute *professionally* to making their show worth watching.

Sure, maybe you're good-looking, funny looking, or evil-looking. But you're also a good actor with a professional work ethic. You're reliable. Easy to work with. Always on time. Know your lines. Take direction well. A good team player.

Be a professional about your work, and producers, directors and casting agents will call you time and again with acting jobs.

PATIENCE: As an acting coach, I've heard just about everything. Like when beginning actors say they want to study for maybe a month, then become a working actor. I try not to laugh.

It may take an actor ten to fifteen years to establish a career—let alone learn to act well.

Look at Johnny Depp. He didn't just appear out of nowhere. I remember seeing his headshot cross my desk a lifetime ago (or so it seems)! I looked at his photo, saw an energy in his eyes and wanted to call him in for a low-budget movie I was casting. But the director, who had pre-screened my choices, wouldn't let me do it.

Anyway, it took Depp twenty years—from his first role in *A Nightmare On Elm Street*—to land his Oscar nomination for *Pirates of the Caribbean*.

It took Brad Pitt "only" fourteen years. He struggled, working as an "extra," in commercials, a small guest star part on the sitcom *Growing Pains*—all this before his breakthrough role in *Thelma and Louise*.

True, miracles happen, and some happen sooner than later. But be prepared to go the long haul. Hone your skills, keep up with your networking and be patient.

PERSISTENCE: Keep moving ahead. If you gain a few pounds, don't hide in your apartment until you lose it.

Instead, go to your acting classes. If you break up with your boyfriend, still make that audition. (Who knows? You might have a crying scene and do the best job ever—and get the part!)

Never wait for perfect conditions or the perfect mood. "Perfect" never happens. Do an attitude check and keep persistently pursuing your career as you continue on your path to success. And remember that a lot of your competition will give up and drop out of sight.

When Clint Eastwood's career wasn't going well in Hollywood, he didn't quit. Instead, he did spaghetti westerns in Europe. He was persistent.

PROACTION: So many clients at my school, The Actor's Edge in Hollywood, are starting careers in late middle age—their fifties and sixties—simply because they postponed their dreams. At least they're finally going for it. For most people, one day leads to a week—which leads to months, which leads to years, which leads to—you guessed it, a lifetime.

So do it *now*. To be proactive is an extraordinary quality. Remember, acting in front of your bedroom mirror doesn't qualify and it won't get you anywhere.

Getting out there, taking risks and feeling a bit uncomfortable or financially pressured is all part of the path of the majority of successful people. So many aspiring actors put off taking acting lessons or getting their new photos taken until there's an easier or more convenient time. If you're aware of many of the life stories of most successful actors, then you know how they struggled, but. . . never waited. . . and never let an opportunity pass them by. They actually went out of their way to achieve taking all of the steps on their path to stardom! Let your motto be, "Do what needs to be done, when it needs to be done!"

POWER OF POSITIVE THINKING: Visualization *is* a powerful force, and it's not the same as dreaming. Jim Carrey used to sit in the Hollywood Hills, think about his soon-to-be successful acting career and even wrote checks to himself for millions of dollars.

So many books are out there on positive thinking. Buy some, read them and take the advice to heart. Put yourself on a mental diet of healthy, uplifting thoughts, and don't let the negative ones eat you up.

One excellent book: *Creative Visualization* by Shatki Gaiwan. Try the workbook version. It might help you build a successful career.

Elvis Presley was a family friend—how's that for name-dropping?—and he once told my sister Sandy about the enormous difference between having ego and having faith. Most people confuse the two, he said. But while ego is simply obnoxious and hard to be around, faith in yourself is an absolute requirement, particularly when they've rejected you ten auditions in a row.

When that happens to you (and it probably will), it doesn't mean you're an incompetent lowlife not worthy of breathing the air. Instead, separate your ego, emotions and insecurities from your job. Maybe, with no callbacks after ten auditions, you might consider honing your acting skills—or simply learn to relax in high-pressure situations. But rejection is never something to take personally.

Stay positive even when life puts you to the test. Forget about audition rejections: What about paying the rent? Utilities? No money for new clothes? Be prepared for the sacrifices you'll make as a scrambling actor. Keep looking for that light at the end of the tunnel.

DITCH THE EGO - BUT KEEP THE FAITH

It's not just *your* mindset that matters, either.

It's the people in your life. So many actors let loved ones sabotage their careers.

For example: Jealous boyfriends or girlfriends who don't like your kissing scenes with a total (and attractive) stranger. Spouses who worry about your intermittent work and irregular paychecks. Parents who want you to be a doctor, lawyer, or corporate drone.

If acting is truly your heart's desire, don't let anyone sour you on it.

When you are a success, the people who gave you the least support will be the first in line to ask for an autograph. (When that happens, give it graciously, and try not to let the smile on your face morph into a smirk.)

YOUR SPIRITUALITY

I've had the privilege of knowing and working with many successful people in the industry, and the vast majority have one major thing in common—their great and unabiding faith in a Higher Power.

Whatever your spiritual beliefs may be—*plug into your power source*.

Be aware of the spirit within you and around you, whatever your concept of God and God-Energy is. Believe in the best and believe in miracles. Pray (frequently). And have a higher purpose above and beyond your acting career.

Some years ago, I had a conversation with the television star Danny Thomas (*Make Room For Daddy*) in his beautiful mansion in Trousdale Estates, perhaps the richest part of the very wealthy community of Beverly Hills. Danny was telling me about the early days of his career as a down-on-his-luck singer and actor.

One fateful day, after reading about St. Jude—the Patron Saint of Hopeless Causes—Danny, desperate for work, with seven dollars in his pocket, prayed for help in "finding his way in life."

From that day on, Danny says, he never stopped working as a singer and an actor.

To him, it was a miracle. Eventually, he became a millionaire, a world-famous celebrity—and kept his pledge to build a shrine to the saint. In 1962, he founded St. Jude Children's Hospital in Memphis.

Today, St. Jude, long acknowledged as one of the world's great research hospitals, has cured thousands of children of catastrophic disease. No family pays for treatment beyond what's covered by insurance.

HAVE A HIGHER PURPOSE, ABOVE AND BEYOND YOUR CAREER

The principal behind the "higher purpose" theory is that the universal energy will help one miraculously along their path if there is a passion towards a larger purpose than just our own selfish goals; helping underprivileged children, abused animals, certain deprived ethnic groups or minorities, human rights issues or the world's environmental needs.

Skill. Clearly, your acting skill is a component of your diamond. That's the *function* of your product. More on this later.

FINANCIAL BASE (YOUR BUDGET)

Think of your financial base as the setting your diamond is in.

It's what keeps the diamond steady, what makes it secure.

If you're lucky enough to have parents or a spouse offering financial support while you take acting lessons and go to auditions, then you're off and running.

But most of us aren't that fortunate. Most aspiring actors need a job to pay the bills while pursuing a career.

Whatever job you take, it must have flexibility. (If your boss threatens to fire you because you're taking time off to audition, then you don't have a flexible job.)

So what do you do? Well—ever see the Neil Simon play, the one where the restaurant customer says not, *"Oh, waiter,"* but *"Oh, actor"?* Waiting on tables and bartending is probably the most common way for actors to support themselves while looking for work. Why? Because if they need to take

MY INITIAL EXPENSES

(Oh My!)

PROFESSIONAL PHOTOGRAPHS

HEADSHOT DUPLICATIONS

RESUMÉ

POSTAGE

ACTING LESSONS

ACTING BOOKS

INSTRUCTIONAL TAPES

DIALECT TAPES / VOICE COACH

SPECIAL PAGER OR CELL PHONE

DEPENDABLE TRANSPORTATION / GAS

VARIED WARDROBE

GROOMING

SUBSCRIPTIONS TO TRADE MAGAZINES

COMPUTER/INTERNET /PRINTER

TV, DVD PLAYER, VCR, CABLE

LESSONS FOR SINGING, DANCING, ETC.

GRAND TOTAL: $

LATER ON, YOU'LL NEED TO INVEST IN THE FOLLOWING...

1. UNION FEES

2. DEMO REELS

3. BUSINESS MEALS

4. BUSINESS GIFTS

5. PROMOTION (PUBLICITY ADS)

off to audition, they simply switch shifts with a colleague (odds are, another actor).

Another way: Do "extra" or background work in movies and television. Not only is there flexibility, you meet other actors, producers, directors, casting people—precisely the types that any aspiring actor *should* meet. As an extra, you may be little more than a fly in the room—but at least you're in the room.

Through osmosis, if nothing else, extras become familiar with production techniques, they see how professional people operate and soon feel like they're a part of the business rather than an outsider.

Extras also get opportunities to do brief (one or two line) speaking parts. And the pay, while it varies from job to job, isn't that bad either.

Other possibilities: Sales work that allows you to set your own hours; freelance writing for local newspapers and magazines; or, if you're certified, personal training at a local gym. You've heard the stories. Harrison Ford was a part-time carpenter, Jim Carrey did janitorial work.

While bringing in the money, you've got to budget how it goes out. Money spent on your acting career is a priority. And it's not cheap. Here's the often hard-to-take news: *If you really want to be a working actor*, you'll probably have to invest thousands of dollars to get your career off to a good start.

Prioritize your expenses. If it's a European vacation or your career—choose career, if you're really serious about this.

If you're considering spending money on your career— and decide that you "can't afford it"– maybe you're really saying, "I won't afford it." If that's the case, you need to re-think.

To get money back, you've got to put it in.

Actually, when you look at the millions that actors can make in the industry, the ratio of investment money to potential income is small. But at the beginning of your career, it may look like quite a sacrifice.

WATCH OUT—SCAMS

There are so many people out there who want to take advantage of you. And it's tough, separating the good guys from the bad, but here are a few things you can bank on.

You never pay an agent "upfront money" to represent you. A reputable agent works off commission.

Agents and managers are not your acting coaches or pho-tographers. That's a conflict of interest.

They also should not insist that you go to a particular act-ing coach or photographer. If they do, you can assume there is a big chance that they are getting kickbacks for sending you.

Screen Actors Guild rules say agents can only charge a 10% commission on your earnings for a union job, and also 20% commission on your earnings for a non-union job (unions, meaning SAG, AFTRA and AEA; see the section on unions for more information). Also, this only applies to jobs you have obtained within their category of represent-ing you.

One exception: "extra" casting agents do charge a regis-tration fee to handle you. This is regarded as perfectly acceptable practice. You can trust extra agencies like Central Casting, on the West Coast—they're quality, they're the biggest and they've been around forever. An East Coast branch of Central Casting is opening in 2006. Or Bill Dance Casting, another top-notch outfit on the West Coast. Ron Howard works with Bill all the time. Also on the West Coast, I've been hearing good things about L.A. Extras and Vision Casting.

STEP 2

ACTING SKILLS

Have Them

Fill in the blank:

Doctors go to med school; attorneys go to law school; actors go to

_____

Insert one of the following phrases into the above sentence:

A) ACTING SCHOOL

B) THE UNEMPLOYMENT LINE

Get the point?

As a working child-actor, starring on Broadway, in movies and on network television, I took this as a given. Every working actor I've ever known, knows this. As a casting director, virtually everyone I see on auditions knows this.

But as an acting coach, I meet many aspiring actors who don't know this.

I pity them. Boats float. Computers compute. And actors *should* act.

No matter how great a product looks on the outside, it must *function* to be a marketable item.

No matter how much you're in this for the money, or to make Mom and Dad proud, or to show your ex just how special you really are—make very sure you're in this *because you have a passion for the art of acting.*

You will continue to study the art of acting even as a working actor. You'll continue to grow until you leave the stage of this world—or just the stage.

Sir Lawrence Olivier, arguably the greatest stage actor who ever lived, continued to study up until the day before he died.

Acting skills can be divided into main groups—*Concept* and *Performance*.

Concept is your ability to pick up a scene from a script, and by your choices, make a comedy more comedic. Or a drama more dramatically moving. This is known as *Scene Breakdown Technique*. At the Actor's Edge studio, I teach the theory in one evening. But you'll practice, develop and refine your scene breakdown technique for the rest of your acting career.

Concept also includes your *audition technique* and *mindset*— that is, knowing what goes on during the audition process and what's required of you as an actor. Also practicing your auditioning so you become more comfortable with the process.

If I could hand you a treasure to take with you on auditions, it would be these two sentences:

GO TO GIVE THE GIFT.
DON'T GO TO GET THE GIFT.

In other words, the more you worry about getting the job, the more nervous you'll become during auditions. The more nervous you are, the less effective you'll be.

Instead, simply go to give your talent, your passion and your skills. Give them the product—you.

And don't forget to have fun. I had the great privilege of working as a casting director for Chuck Barris, the genius game show writer-producer (*The Dating Game*, *The Newlywed Game*, *The Gong Show*, a bunch more). To this day, I don't think Chuck knows how much I learned from him. He became a billionaire, partly because he understood the business, partly because he grasped the principles of creation.

Grasped and never let go. Chuck used to say, "Chris, if it's not fun, we won't do it." He knew you had to enjoy what you're doing so others can enjoy watching you. That's all a matter of attitude, of course, but I can tell you this: The more you study acting, the more acting skills you have; the more acting skills you have, the more fun the audition process becomes.

Performance skills are those things that allow you to play your emotional instrument intensely and believably. Like how to cry on cue. Or be angry. Or laugh out loud.

Here's a thumbnail sketch:

METHOD ACTING: A performance skill developed by Constantine Stanislavsky. It is based on relaxation technique and a series of exercises which develop your ability to bring forth, on cue and believably, the emotions called for in a scene. Method can be divided into two major components: "sense memory" and "affective memory." Using past memories of what an actor experienced emotionally and with their five senses, a method actor can cry effortlessly, on cue along with any other emotional state required as well, and be believable in any scene.

I worked on Broadway, in New York with some excellent method actors, and I can tell you that the work they put into preparation paid off tremendously in standing ovations for us all!

MEISNER TECHNIQUE: Another series of exercises designed to bring intense emotions to the surface, developed by Sanford Meisner. The "Repetition Exercises" are designed to hone your skills in listening and observing more intensely, and also to respond more honestly "in the moment."

Both Method and Meisner have the same goals, to get you out of your head and into your heart (or emotions). To which will you respond better? I suggest you learn—and use—both.

COMEDY TECHNIQUE is psychologically-based, whereas drama is emotionally-based. Comedy technique is made up of formulas that you can learn just like "one plus one equals two." Some comedy formulas are:

ADDING CHARACTER FLAWS (perfection is awesome, but flaws are funny)

REPETITION (the three rule—repeat something three or four times, and the last time with a twist)

THE SET-UP AND THE PUNCH LINE (every joke and every comedic story is made of this)

THE RULE OF HOSTILITY, REBELLION AND AGGRESSION (someone is hostile; someone rebels and bends the rules and gets aggressive, like the Keystone Cops throwing pies in each other's faces)

VULNERABILITY (a vulnerable character is funny)

TIMING (this is the rhythm of the scene and also comedic pauses which have to be not too long or too short, and at the right moments)

MISCOMMUNICATION (a funny device which has been used through the ages. Check out the classic routine of "Who's On First" by Abbott and Costello).

There is so much more to learn but you will. . . and you will have lots of fun doing so!

Most important, don't forget that comedy needs to be clear in order for the audience to psychologically "get" the joke.

IMPROVISATIONAL TECHNIQUE is the ability to be *in the moment* during every second of your performance. Whether you're performing totally without a script and making it up as you go, or using improv as a supplement to a scripted scene, it's a mandatory technique of the working actor.

There are definite rules to improvisation. Most of the rules of setting up improvisations will teach you about what the most important elements of scripted scenes are (how to set up a scene) and also get you in the habit of working with the other actors, accepting their contributions and responding to them. Even though improvisation is a technique of performing while not using a script, it helps prepare an actor for being more spontaneous within scripted scene work and to approach their scripted scene performances with more confidence and a spirit of more spontaneity and independently creative thinking.

Combine the two and we get **COMEDY IMPROV**—my favorite class to teach because it's so much fun to learn. The energy in the room is tremendous!

DRAMATIC IMPROV utilizes the rules of improvisation once again. The difference—the subject matter is dramatic. Here you will learn the elements of drama and will use them to move the audience emotionally. One major requirement is believability. You must give a believable performance or the audience will not be moved.

NOTE: To have power as an actor, you must know the elements of comedy and drama, and learn how to see them and bring them out in a scene. The actor goes beyond the creation that the writer wrote. The writer simply does the sketch on the canvas. The actor paints the colors and textures, hopefully with *passion*. I always say a good actor can take a dramatic scene and make it a comedy, but a bad actor can take a comedic scene and make it a tragedy!

COMMERCIAL TECHNIQUE is a specific formula for acting in commercials: Learning how to hold and display product (more to it than it sounds) and giving a proper pitch. But it's not a substitute for learning how to act.

ON-CAMERA TECHNIQUE is very different from performing onstage. Terminology is different, and learning proper blocking techniques (movement choreography) is critical.

COLD READING AND AUDITION TECHNIQUES are very important so that you can ace your acting auditions and get the jobs! No matter how well you know the other acting techniques, you must be able to adapt your performances to the audition arena. What to say to a casting director, how to "schmooze them" without seeming obvious, the etiquette of the audition, how to prepare yourself for the performance *under pressure* are all extremely valuable techniques that you need to know to be a working actor.

VOICEOVER TECHNIQUE is what you must learn if you are planning to be "off camera" talent. The stars of the voiceover world are the voices that you hear on radio, television and even a ride at a theme part like Disneyland—but you never see their faces. This very lucrative field could have you driving around in a limousine and flying around in a private jet, while your name is well-known only to the voiceover industry professionals and not the general public.

The major catch is that it's very hard to break into at first and to get a voiceover agent. Also you must have a professional voiceover CD before you can start working. When I was 12, I remember doing a voiceover for a cartoon movie for California-based Hanna-Barbera. It still airs every year at Christmas time and the residuals (money you get every time it is shown) were tremendous!

Memorization techniques *actually do exist. Since memorizing scripts are a big part of an actor's job, if you find yourself having a difficult time remembering lines, you can turn to the many books, tapes and nutritional supplements which can help you memorize more easily.*

Relaxation technique *is, in my opinion, the most important technique that an actor needs. Without being able to relax under pressure, an actor cannot utilize any of the above-mentioned techniques properly, let alone memorize lines. At The Actor's Edge in Hollywood, we actually have a hypnotherapist come in on certain weekends to help teach people how to hypnotize themselves and to relax. It's that important!*

The above paragraphs, of course, barely scratch the surface and are outside the scope of this book and DVD. We're here to teach you more about the business side of being a working actor. But if you want a more in-depth look at these acting skills, purchase one or all of our videotaped series and accompanying books on the subjects listed above.

I urge you to take your studies at acting school very seriously.

That means take notes during class. Do your homework. Practice your scenes. Study movies, TV shows and commercials. And buy acting books. Three sources for them are on the Internet: Samuel French Books, Amazon.com and The Drama Book Shop. I highly recommend them all.

Don't ignore dialect tapes, either. Every actor can benefit from a British, Southern and New York dialect. Choose the rest based on your physical appearance. If you're Latino, you don't necessarily need to have an Asian dialect. If you're Asian, skip the Jamaican dialect.

Conversely, if you normally speak with a foreign dialect, I strongly recommend *Acting With An American Dialect,* by David Allen Stern. His taped series offers every dialect you'll ever need to know.

Remember, it's a ready-made, fast food world: A professional actor has dialects ready to perform, on cue. If a casting director likes several actors equally—equal in looks and acting ability—the ones who get callbacks are those with the additional dialect skills that are required for the particular roles they are auditioning for.

Or, for that matter, those actors with other special skills:

SINGING

DANCING

PLAYING A MUSICAL INSTRUMENT

SPEAKING ANOTHER LANGUAGE

MARTIAL ARTS

ROLLERBLADING

SKATEBOARDING

JUGGLING

SCUBA DIVING

STUNT SKILLS

CPR TRAINING

You never know what extra-special skill they need for the role. So hone them all, add some new ones and keep them sharp. Casting directors greatly prefer actors with a special skill—rather than having to hire a singer (to dub in their singing) or a dancer (to double in dance scenes).

TIPS FOR SUCCESS

Whether millionaire, or billionaire, some of the greatest treasures of knowledge I can share with you, are those I've learned from successful producers and industry people I've known.

WINK MARTINDALE

Be on time.

Use good manners, & etiquette.

Arise early. You'll accomplish a lot!

Live clean and love God.

Be neat, clean, and organized.

Anything doing is worth doing very well.

CHUCK BARRIS (producer)

Have fun while you're working.

Be playful while you're working!

Don't be afraid to let your inner child create.

Every project should contain comedy, drama, and sex, no matter
  what genre.

SANDY MARTINDALE (co-producer of The 7 Steps to Stardom)

Don't give up. Keep trying and you'll do it!

Value your friendships. Support each other.

With God, all things are possible!

Don't be afraid to walk up to anybody . . . and make new friends.

Believe in yourself, go forward with confidence, and you'll succeed.

Dress well.

TONY FERRA (self-made millionaire/celebrity nightclub owner)

Work hard and make work a priority, to succeed.

Arise early.

Too much time off from work causes loss.

Every business and product should have a strong and identifiable theme.

Put your earnings into real estate investments.

Pray.

Don't let anybody tell you that you can't do it. Anything is possible.

BOB WALL (producer, and CEO of the Worldwide Black Belt Association)

Every "no" leads to a "yes."

Don't quit until you succeed.

In any business, be a great salesman.

Be disciplined. Live a clean wholesome life.

Exercise hard, daily, and keep healthy.

ELVIS PRESLEY

Have faith that what you want to do for a living, comes from God's will.

Believe that with all your heart.

Perform without ego and without fear of failing. Just do it for God.

DAVID WINTERS (producer)

Learn everything about your industry.

Don't be afraid to start at the bottom.

Don't be afraid to work jobs beneath your goals, while on your path to success.

Have patience, and a plan that you stick to.

In production and writing, distribution contacts are key.

ALAN BAILEY (VP, Paramount Pictures)

Know the industry you're working in, thoroughly.

Don't forget to be kind and help others along the way.

If writing a movie, lower budget movies make more profit.

BILL DANCE (Casting Director)

Act with passion.

Be real. Be vulnerable.

Work hard at your craft.

Being good looking isn't enough.

Be professional and have good manners.

STEP 3

YOUR PHOTOGRAPH

The Essence of the Product

The key to the casting director's door—and your future agent's door—is the actor's photograph. (Also known as the "headshot.")

As part of the pre-screening process of actors, we almost always view the actor's photograph and resumé before agreeing to see them for an interview or an audition.

There is no reason whatsoever to take photos if you don't know *why* you're taking the picture.

What are you trying to show us?

Advertisers place a photo of a bowl of soup in a magazine to show the product can *function*.

That way, when shopping in the market, you look at the soup can and think:

The soup looks like it can nourish my body.

Just look at all those veggies.

Looks like it's tasty, too.

Or when shopping for a pair of jeans:

The jeans look like they fit well.

They will make me look good.

The soup nourishes—the jeans wear well.

A *photo of an actor must show the product can function—i.e., that the product can act.*

If you get this, you're already well beyond many aspiring actors who spend their entire photo session hiding their laugh lines or fixing their hair, rather than showing they can emote.

How do you show that you can act—with a photograph? After all, the casting director can't hear you talk or see you move.

It's all in the eyes.

It's all in the eyes.

It's all in the eyes.

Your eyes should show great intensity. Emotional intensity. An energy, deeply expressing the emotion you are feeling, *must* permeate the photo. When that happens—*Wham!*—you catch the casting director's attention above and beyond the *thousands* of other photos they see.

You need two types of headshots: The *theatrical* shot and the *commercial* shot. The theatrical shot is dramatic, hence it's submitted for any movie, theatre or TV role that's dramatic. Your commercial shot is comedic and joyful, so it goes for any movie, theatre or TV role that's comedic, and also for most commercial roles.

During the taking of the theatrical shot, be dramatic with specificity. To put it another way, focus on sex—or anger. These are the two strong choices for a dramatic shot. Let the sexiness or rage show through your eyes. To intensify your look, here's a secret: Angle your chin slightly down, then look up to the side ever so slightly.

Look closely at the two pictures of actor David Jordan on page 42-43.

In the "before" picture—one of David's photos from his first commercial shot—look at the eyes. There's a lack of emotion. A lack of joy. Not just his eyes, either, but his smile too. In turn, agents and casting directors expressed a lack of interest.

Now look at the "after" picture. Way better. David's eyes show a sexy intensity. This picture did generate interest.

DAVID A. JORDAN

DAVID A. JORDAN

Same actor. Different pics. Different results.

Now look at Andrew Mullin's shots on pages 46-47. Look at the one on the left, and see how Andrew's eyes are looking straight on, dead-again.

Compare it to the one on the right, taken later. In this shot, Andrew's angling his eyes up, and he looks much more intense—a much more interesting shot. Do you see the difference in the eyes?

Rent the classic rock movie *Purple Rain* and watch how Prince uses his eyes and angles them up in almost every scene. (Speaking of rock music—if it gets you in the mood to emote, as music often does—play it during your session).

During the taking of the commercial shot, smile and laugh with all of your heart and soul. Don't worry about wrinkles or imperfect teeth. The joy should show through your eyes. Never waste a shot with dead eyes and a phony smile. Be uninhibited, ask the photographer to tell jokes (or at least try to loosen you up) and work into your happy emotional state. Actor David Dortch's excellent commercial shot appears at right.

DAVID DORTCH

Don't be stiff or posed. Don't stand in an uncomfortable position. Did you ever see those Chamber of Commerce type pictures in the local paper, with everyone standing in front of a building, ramrod straight with fixed smiles? Or the

TYSON RUSSELL

This shot is too posed.

This one is much better.
It shows a sexy intensity
in the eyes.

group picture in your school yearbook? Those are not the kind of photos that will market you. Relax and be you.

All headshots are 8 x 10 inches and shot in color or black and white, whatever the current trend indicates. Of course, if you shoot in color, you can still duplicate in black and white.

You can take headshots, tight shots of just your face, or shots from the shoulders up. You can also take full body shots or ¾ length shots. I suggest taking all of the above.

Beginners should take at least three rolls of photos if the photographer is using film. In digital photography terms (since there are no rolls of film), that's roughly 70 to 90 shots.

For your first few sessions, and until you're a strong actor, it may take a few frames to warm into emotions and attitudes. Advanced actors, when they update their photos, usually get what they want from a one-roll photo session, or in digital photography terms, 24 to 36 photos.

ANDREW MULLIN

ANDREW MULLIN

Most professional photographers offer hair and make-up with your session for an extra fee. That's fine, but it must still look like you; so wear your hair and make-up pretty much the way you usually do. *No false advertising*—no glamour shots and no airbrushing. When you walk into the casting office, no one should say, "Where's your younger sister? Y'know—*the one in this picture?!?*"

Nothing in the photo should distract us from you. No attention-grabbing backgrounds. No jewelry, no hats, no busy prints, no logos, and as a general rule, no props. Only solid colors for your clothes.

For your initial session, you'll take pictures in three types of outfits. One is your corporate look. In the 1950s, this was a tuxedo or evening gown. Today, it's simply a good suit.

The second outfit is your upscale casual look. For younger people, that's jeans and an open collar or T-shirt; for the more mature, slacks with an open-collar shirt. Please note the example photos below of Dr. Boris Bagdassarroff.

BORIS BAGDASSARROFF

Corporate Look   His upscale casual look

GENE GILMORE

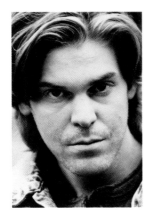 

Your career course can change with a different hairstyle or even a different collar. On the left, Gene Gilmore wears unkempt hair and a frayed collar. It's a good photo for a "bad guy" part. But on the right, Gene has groomed hair, a white collar, a stylish leather jacket plus an illumination of light focused toward his eyes. This photo earned Gene an audition for a romantic lead in a soap opera.

Your third look is something that fits your specialty—whatever is uniquely you. That could be the nerdy professor with glasses and a highly conservative outfit. It might be the bad guy in the T and leather jacket. Maybe it's the comedian with bright-colored clothing that breaks all the rules—something just plain wacko. You may want to take several character shots wearing different outfits.

If you have facial hair (I'm speaking only to the men on this one!), take your pictures just the way you usually look. Don't send out pictures of a clean-shaven man and then enter the casting office with a full beard.

If you cut your hair, grow your hair, change its color, get older-looking or younger-looking, reshoot your photos.

If you wear glasses all the time, keep them on in your pictures. If they're optional, take some pictures without them, and your character picture with them.

Be choosy when shopping for a photographer. Look at their samples. Did they light the other actors well? Are they in focus? Are the people posed or do they look natural? And check out the cost. What do they charge per session? How many photos do you get per session? Do they charge extra for proofs? How much do they charge extra for each photo that you blow-up? Do they keep your negatives or photo CD, or do you? Do they use a professional still camera or do they use a digital camera and give you the photos on computer disc? Please call around to current photographers to compare prices in your area.

Once you've chosen your photographer: Make sure you (politely) *lead the session*. As an actor, you have the right to do this. Tell the photographer what you want to achieve. Make certain they comply.

If a position feels posed and uncomfortable, tell them and do something that feels more natural for you. If they want to shoot outdoors, fine. But if the sun is in your eyes, making you squint (and, without a doubt, making you look horrible), tell them you want to move to another location or do indoor shots. Take control.

If your photography session was shot on film, ask for proof rolls instead of proof sheets. Rolls are larger and it makes it easier to choose the best shots. If your photography session was shot with a digital camera, then the photographer has your photos on computer CD and you can get a full screen slide show to review your shots. You can even print out your photos from the disc, if you have the proper kind of printer that turns out great photo prints.

Remember, choose the photos that reveal you at your most intense.

Next step is duplication. For this, you need a professional photo duplication lab, unless you have your session on computer disc, and have purchased the proper computer and printer which prints out quality photos. Do you want black and white or color, according to the current photo trend?

Glossy, matte, pearl and semi-gloss are just a few of the terms used to describe "shiny photos" or "not." Decide what you want and then make sure you are clear on the terms that your local duplication lab is using. Of course, that is unless you have your own computer and printer. Then all you have to do is choose the correct premium quality photo paper that you desire (which is "shiny" or "not.")

Do you want a border around your photo with your name on it, or no border at all with your name "bled" on the bottom? If you do want a border, what font style and size do you want for your name? There's really no right or wrong for any of this—it's all a matter of personal choice.

You also have a choice in the duplication process. Lithographic, photographic or laser print on photographic paper? Check out all three processes and choose what makes the clearest copies. Just make sure it's not grey or grainy.

I suggest one single shot per photograph. Composites, which go in and out of fashion, tend to confuse the casting director. Are you the smiling clean-cut person or the bad guy with the mean look? Don't send them both for the same role.

Once again, watch out for scams. Many photographers are lousy and unprofessional: You'll end up with something resembling a passport picture. It's also not uncommon to hear actors complain about photographers asking them to take their shirt off or pose in sexy lingerie. Don't let that happen to you. That's sexual harassment.

Zed cards—two or four-sided photo composites—are really only for models, or actors who also model. Please refer to Nathan Luginbill's zed card on the right. Only get them if you're doing print work. They can cost thousands of dollars, so don't let a photographer talk you into getting a Zed unless you require it because you are also intending on modeling and doing print jobs.

There are photographers who use a defined-focus lens, which *emphasizes* your facial lines. Then they refer you to an airbrushing lab, where you pay big bucks to get the wrinkles out of the picture. The photographer gets a kickback. If they try this with you, report them to the Better Business Bureau or whatever its equivalent in your area. Also, if you haven't paid in full yet—don't. Try insisting that they reshoot with a more flattering lens at no additional charge. If they refuse to work it out with you, take them to small claims court to get your money back.

Always keep in mind that your photos are your primary marketing tools for your product—you. So make them fantastic! If the first session doesn't work, keep reshooting until

NATHAN
LUGINBILL

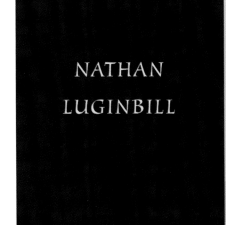

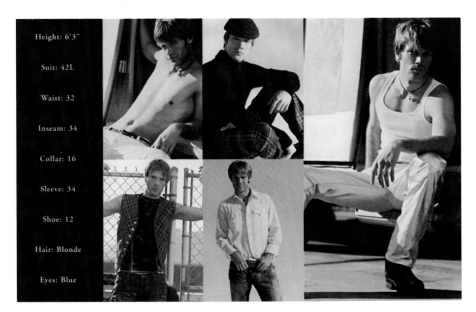

Height: 6'3"

Suit: 42L

Waist: 32

Inseam: 34

Collar: 16

Sleeve: 34

Shoe: 12

Hair: Blonde

Eyes: Blue

you get the "magic picture." (You'll know the "magic picture" because you will receive a lot of positive responses from casting directors and agents by submitting it to them.)

STEP 4

YOUR RESUMÉ

The Label on the Product

Here are the initial stages of the casting process:

A producer hires a casting director—like me—to cast a film, TV pilot or play. I read the script and meet with the producer, director or anyone else involved with casting.

Before the meeting, I do my homework and complete a preliminary character breakdown of the script, listing all principal roles in the project along with descriptions gleaned from the script.

I also write additional descriptions, including age range and any special abilities required of the actors. I note which parts should be name actors, also called "draw names" because they draw the public in (based on the budget).

Then the meeting: It gives me even more clarity on the casting.

Then I put out the official *breakdown*. The definitive listing of all roles to be filled and a complete description of individual characters. I indicate if I'm looking for a star name, or if I can use an unknown to fill the role.

The next day, the breakdown notices go to *hundreds* of agents. On that day (in Hollywood at least), my list qualifies as a best seller.

The agents read them and decide which actors they represent are right for which parts.

Then they submit headshots to my casting office for consideration.

I might receive as many as 2,000 photographs for one role. This deserves repeating:

2,000 PHOTOGRAPHS FOR ONE ROLE!

By the time you read this, the number may be higher, since so many join the profession every day. You can understand then, with time of the essence, how distressingly easy it is to quickly toss away 1,900 of the photos to find 100 with intensity. (Now you see how important your photos are!)

With those 100 pictures, I turn them over on the desk, face down. Then I read the resumés on the back. This is, of course, if they are submissions delivered by mail or by messenger. If they are emailed, I click on the resumés when I like the pictures.

I keep the best 50 and call them in to audition.

You could be one of those 50.

But not if your resumé stands in the way.

Your resumé is the label on the product. It tells casting directors, producers and agents the names of the consumers who've used the product, what special features go with the product and the training that went into preparing the product to function.

Just like the can of soup. If you picked one up at the supermarket, looked at the label and saw items scratched out, extra ingredients scribbled in and words misspelled, would you buy it? Don't think so.

Same with casting directors. We expect an actor's resumé to be neat, with correct spelling and printed on a computer. An actor's resumé is a marketing tool, second in importance only to the headshot.

You must follow the actor's format for resumés. It's different from all other professions.

For starters: Your resumé should be cut from letter-sized to 8 x 10 so it fits perfectly on the back of your picture. It must be stapled on the four corners back-to-back with your photo.

It's possible to print out resumés on the back of photos—but if you have a service that takes your picture and prints hundreds of resumés this way, you'll have to throw away those pictures when you update your resumé. (And you always update when you get a new acting job or take a new acting class.)

The color of your resumé doesn't have to be white. A different, more eye-catching color is okay. You can also watermark your resumé with another picture of yourself scanned on it.

There's a sample resumé coming up. But I'd like to emphasize the following:

Your name is placed boldly on the top of your resumé (much larger than other types of job resumés). If starting your career in America, please check with Screen Actors Guild to make sure that some other working actor isn't already registered with SAG under the same name as yours. If they are there first, you may have to change the spelling of your name, or the entire name. After all, it is a product name in business.

Your statistics go on the left side on the resumé. This means your height, weight, hair color and eye color. Only put your "D.O.B." (date of birth) if you are under 18. After 18 years, you do not put your age. Also do not put your social security number, clothing sizes or home addresses.

Your contact information goes on the right side of the

resumé. This is where you put your business phone number and also your e-mail address and website info, if you have one. Once you have agency representation, their contact information will go here.

Your credits will be listed within the categories they are in. Some of those categories are: *Film, Television, Videos, Industrials/DVDs, Commercials, Theatre* and *Live Venue*. Other categories after your credits will be *Training* and *Special Skills*. When on the West Coast in the U.S., *Theatre* goes last on the credit list. When on the East Coast, *Theatre* goes first.

All of your categories for credits are for principle acting roles. Never say "principle" or "extra" on your resumé, as it is assumed they are all principle acting roles. Extras do not need resumés.

Never lie. It's false advertising and will only get you into trouble.

Never put dates on your credits. Put your best and strongest credits first.

Only list a category of credit if you have one or more credits within that particular category already. Otherwise, leave it off until a future date.

Throughout the categories of work credits are three neat columns, evenly distributed across the page of your resumé.

In column one, list the name of the show. If it's a music video, in this column, you would list the name of the artist or band.

In the middle column, list the size or type of role you played. I've seen the middle column listed two different ways. You can list the size of the roles you play, such as lead, co-lead, supporting (throughout the majority of the project but not starring or co-starring), cameo (starring in one or just a few scenes), featured (a very small part), guest star (for TV), or recurring (being a guest star on a TV show more than once).

The other version of the middle column format is to list the characters you played, such as waiter, bartender, president or doctor. People usually exercise this latter version when they have only featured parts. Makes sense: By listing everything as a "featured part," the resumé looks like mostly "extra" work and that diminishes the credibility of the principle roles that you have played.

How do you decide if a role is a featured principle role or just simply an extra part? Well, if you're in a crowd with everyone running from the T-Rex, but you slip and fall and he decides to eat *you*, and we see you turn to face him just before he crunches down on you—well, lucky you, that's a featured part, and you're an established actor. Congratulations, and put that one on your resumé.

Even if your part ends up on the cutting room floor, list the credit. After all, you were hired for the part and paid to do it.

In the third column, list the production company that your show was produced by, such as CBS or Dreamworks. Some people list the directors they worked under in that column as well. I suggest not to leave the production company off.

A change in format is as follows for commercials: Do not list the commercials that you've done. Simply put "List available on request," or "Conflicts upon request." Nobody needs to see the list. If you are hired to do a Coca Cola commercial, you will be asked if there are any conflicts. Are you currently on TV in another soda commercial for one of their competitors? A verbal response is all that is required.

If you are a beginner and your resumé looks a little lean, there are ways to fill it up. List acting training, special classes and seminars. The less credits on your resumé, the more acting training that should be listed. Do student films at local colleges and universities. They appear the same as regular films, so don't say "student film," just the title, role and name of the student's made-up production company. Fill in all of your special skills.

Moving down the page of your resumé, we now fill in the category of "Training." This does not mean training to be a veterinarian or a doctor. This category applies to acting training. List the various acting skills you've studied on separate lines and in three columns. In the first column, what skill you studied; in the second column, what school; and in the third, what teacher. Instead of listing the first column like this:

ACTING

List the first column this way:

SCENE BREAKDOWN TECHNIQUE

COMEDY IMPROVISATION

COMMERCIAL TECHNIQUE

After your acting training, you may list *only* these other areas of training:

SINGING

DANCING

MUSICAL INSTRUMENTS

STAGE COMBAT OR STUNT TRAINING

The last category on the page is "Special Skills." List your special skills across the page headed by a category title like Languages, Dialects, Singing, Dancing, Musical Instruments, Sports, Awards, Modeling, Misc.

When you list special skills, don't put down activities you can't do reasonably well. If you list swimming, you don't have to be Olympic-caliber, but you shouldn't need water wings either. And don't list things that should be obvious. "Works well with children" is one of them. I hope you don't slap the little kids around!

And one trick that always works. If you don't have many credits, increase your font size.

Nothing wrong with that. Just fill up that page.

On the following page is a sample resumé. Remember, if you don't have a lot of or any credits or training yet, at least you can put your name, stats, contact info and special skills.

SAMPLE RESUMÉ

NAME
UNION AFFILIATION

Height:
Weight:
Eyes: Your Eye Color
Hair: Hair Color

CONTACT NUMBER
OR AGENCY STICKER

FILM:

| (Title) | (Part Played) | (Production Co.) |
| (Title) | (Part Played) | (Production Co.) |

TELEVISION:

| (Title) | (Part Played) | (Production Co.) |
| (Title) | (Part Played) | (Production Co.) |

COMMERCIALS: LIST AVAILABLE ON REQUEST

THEATRE:

| (Show Title) | (Part Played) | (Production Co.) |

EDUCATION / TRAINING:

| (School) | (Technique Studied) | (Location) |

SPECIAL SKILLS: (Dialects, Sing/Dance/Instruments, Athletics)

STEP 5

YOUR AGENT

The Marketing Rep for the Product

Your agent is your first, most important relationship in your business.

They submit your photos and resumés for movie, television, theatre and commercial jobs. They connect you to casting directors and production companies and secure auditions. Once you get the job, they negotiate your fee and travel arrangements.

In the U.S., Screen Actors Guild rules govern specifically how many agents may represent an actor. Rules can differ in each state, so check with your local SAG branch. But in most states, an actor may only be represented by one of each type of agent per "area of representation" within a SAG branch jurisdiction. Here are the four areas:

THEATRICAL (for film and TV)

COMMERCIALS

VOICE-OVERS

MODELING / PRINT WORK

(As mentioned earlier, "extra" agents are a different mold. They represent you for background work in movies, TV and commercials, charge an upfront fee for their work and often represent the producer in a project.)

But a legitimate SAG agent can't charge any upfront fees. Generally, the agent charges 10% (20% for non-union jobs) of the jobs you earn within their contractual area of representation.

Agents work for large agencies and boutique (smaller) agencies. The larger ones usually have theatrical, commercial, voice-over and modeling/print departments. Sometimes, one agent will represent you in all these areas, i.e., "across the board."

Some agencies specialize: Athletes who act, stand-up comedians who act, handicapped actors, children, character actors, ethnic groups. Some handle only star names.

To find an agency that's right for you, I suggest *The Agencies*, an excellent book offering an enormous amount of information about specific agencies in your area.

Another way to categorize agencies: The A, B and C list.

A,B,C THE LEGIT AGENTS

F "THE FAKES"

And the F agents, otherwise known as "the fakes."

Now you won't find a book that actually grades agencies this way.

But basically, the A agencies are the very large and successful outfits that handle mostly star names (International

Creative Management and the William Morris Agency are two.) Not only do they represent actors—they also handle producers, directors and writers.

The A's handle most of the stars you know and love, and wheel and deal multi-million dollar contracts for their clients.

I already know what you're thinking. *If you, an unknown actor, could somehow be repped by one of these powerful agencies, your career could take off.*

And though that's a very difficult proposition—it *is* true that some powerhouse agencies have signed unknowns. The term is known as "hip-pocketed," when a super agent who normally represents major movie stars keeps an unknown talent in their "hip pocket" and works on them as a project.

But the requirements to be "hip-pocketed" are very strong. You must have the right look, excellent acting skills, union membership, a strong resumé and perhaps a demo reel available.

You also have to be seen somewhere by one of these agents—or referred by an actor, casting director or other industry person they trust. Agents of this stripe rarely look at mailed-in photo submissions of actors.

So to begin with, B agents are probably the first you should try.

Nothing wrong with that. B's are reputable agencies that handle some celebrity actors and lots of quality actors, perhaps unknown—but who work a lot. They're smaller than "A" agencies, handle fewer actors and often don't have a variety of departments. But they're generally well-connected with a limited number of casting directors and production companies.

It's not easy to get into a B agency either. Union membership is usually required, along with the strong look, strong resumé and excellent acting skills. But B's almost always look at the photos and resumés you submit by mail, and at least consider you for representation.

If you can't get the B agent—try the C's. They represent no star names; instead, they handle actors at the beginning of their careers, submitting them for smaller parts in TV shows, movies and commercials.

The C's don't have much clout. Their connections with casting directors and production companies are limited, aside from submitting your photos after reviewing the breakdowns. But their prerequisites for representation are easier to meet. With them, it's okay if you're still learning to act, as long as you keep taking lessons. They also represent actors not yet union members, and those with little or no resumé credits.

Now drop down a few thousand feet and meet the F agents. The unsavory scam artists.

Unfortunately, they've managed to hide themselves throughout the otherwise reputable B and C categories. The F's scam actors into thinking they'll represent them, but with a few catches.

Like recommending a particular acting school, or using a particular photographer. The actor, of course, dutifully does what the F agent says, and spends hundreds or even thousands of dollars. The agent gets a kickback from the school or the photographer, raking in the dough with no intention whatsoever of really representing the actor.

This scenario plays out in miserable fashion, as the actor waits and waits for the agent's call—a call that never happens. No auditions, nothing.

SAG tries to protect actors from scams, and will close down a scam agency if they are SAG-franchised, and if they can prove it.

Trouble is, it's hard to prove.

After all, *every* agent probably has a favorite photographer and acting school. And it's certainly common practice for a completely reputable agent to tell actors they need more acting lessons or better headshots. It's only natural, then, that the agent recommend his favorites, but not because they're getting a kickback—but only because they know a good photographer or good acting school that enhances your marketability.

So how do you tell the difference between an honest agent simply trying to help you—and the F agent?

Well, try the following. When the agent tells you to get better headshots, say, "Sure, I'll do that. But I can't go to the photographer you suggested. I've already paid a large amount in advance to another professional photographer." Or, "I've already paid a year in advance to a different acting school than the one you suggested. Will you still represent me?"

The F agent will say no—or if he says yes, then disappears and you never hear from him again. The "real" agent will understand.

So now you've determined what agencies you're going to approach. . . . . . What's Next??

Well, don't walk into an agency without an appointment, or call the agent out-of-the-blue to get an appointment. Try that, and they'll do everything short of calling out the National Guard.

Here are the four ways to seek agency representation:

MARRY ONE. Not recommended.

DO "MAILERS." Submit your headshot and resumé along with a brief cover letter addressed to the agent and ask for representation. Stick to a one paragraph letter if you can. They never read long letters.

"SHOWCASE" FOR AGENTS. They attend these showcases, offered by acting schools, the union and various seminars. Here you have a captive audience, just sitting there, waiting to watch you perform and later receive your headshot and resumé.

"PIGGYBACK" another actor you know, and ask them to set up an appointment for you through referral.

Once you've got the appointment, be prepared. Bring your headshots, resumé, proof sheets and demo reel. Have two monologues ready, one comedic and one dramatic. Also be ready to do a cold reading. That's a script they hand you cold, with little or no time to prepare or memorize.

Never say anything negative. Don't trash anyone. Instead of telling them the last director you worked with was a jerk, say "that director was a stimulating challenge."

During a showcase at my school, an advanced actor did a

great audition for an agent—so great, in fact, the agent wanted to represent him. They talked, and somewhere in the conversation he told her that "he didn't get a callback" on his last five auditions.

This made the agent think twice, apparently; she decided not to represent him.

Agents are not confessors, psychologists, or parental figures. They are your marketing representatives. So focus on getting them excited about the product (you) that's going to make so much money (for both of you).

If you're not a member of the Screen Actors Guild, you'll probably be represented by a commercial agent only, or by the commercial department of an agency, until you get one union commercial. Then they will "Taft-Hartley" you into SAG. Once this happens—then and only then—will an agent bother to submit you for TV and movies.

In my advanced class, I have a terrific actor, Ricardo Herranz. He was a soap star in Venezuela (starring in over 4,000 episodes)! You'd think with that kind of a track record, plus his strong romantic-lead look and excellent acting skills, he'd have no problem securing representation from an A agency.

Think again. There's no SAG in Venezuela. So, despite all his experience, Ricardo was, by definition, a non-union actor when he relocated to the United States. When he joined my school, there he was, a diamond of a product lost in a heap of zirconias because of that one common denominator.

Immediately, I called a dynamic agent and friend of mine, Fred Wostbrook, who has encyclopedia-like knowledge of the industry. He suggested I refer Ricardo to a manager who specializes in hot Latin actors.

The manager instantly signed Ricardo and introduced him to a commercial agency for commercial representation only. Ricardo quickly got a part, received his "Taft-Hartley" into SAG and immediately secured theatrical representation for film and TV by The House of Representatives, an A agency in Hollywood.

Now Ricardo's working his way to stardom in the U.S., just like he did in Venezuela. Already, he was up for a starring part in an Aaron Spelling series and a popular soap in New York. It's just a matter of time now, but he wouldn't be in the mainstream today without a good theatrical agent— and he couldn't have a good theatrical agent without his membership in SAG.

In the States, Screen Actors Guild (the union which protects and governs actors) used to have to approve of and "franchise" an agency before it could be able to exist. Unfortunately, there are now agencies which operate without being "SAG-franchised."

When signing with one of these agents, an actor will not be offered a standard SAG contract, so it benefits an actor to seek legal counsel when offered a non-SAG contract before signing it. Make sure you know what you're getting into. You can check up on any agency and see if they are SAG-franchised by calling your local SAG office and asking.

Getting an agent is one thing. Maintaining an excellent relationship is another. It takes nurturing, time, attention, dependability and positivity. You must accept the fact that you're not the only person that your agent represents, even within your age range and physical description. Others might be submitted for the same acting job that's available.

It's like sibling rivalry. Which actor within the agent's group of ten who *could* be submitted for this role *will be submitted?* Maybe one or two actors, but not all ten. That just isn't done. An agent chooses the one or two clients who seem, somehow, to fit the role best.

Of course, once you're a working actor who's making money for the agent, they'll tend to submit you for roles constantly. But until then, what can you do to stand out to your agent—and above the rest of your competition within the agency? Here are some words of wisdom:

FIRST, ALWAYS BE DEPENDABLE.

SHOW UP FOR EVERY AUDITION THE AGENT BOOKS FOR YOU.

ALWAYS BE ON TIME.

RETURN YOUR AGENT'S CALL WITHIN THE HOUR.

Never turn down an audition the agent has booked for you. If you're ill, going out of town, or unavailable for any reason, call the agent in advance. (Don't forget to call when you're available again.)

Stay on their minds—but not on their nerves. No agent likes a pest who takes up too much time. Especially when they're busy. On the other hand, nobody remembers the silent, near invisible individual—those slowly fade from consciousness. Be wise and logical, and tread that fine line.

Each agent has different preferences, so ask if it's all right to call them once a week to touch base and keep current, just three to five minutes, that's all.

When you call, make sure it's after 1:30 in the afternoon, after they've done morning casting submissions and calls, and after they've had lunch—they're less likely to be grouchy then. It's probably best not to call Mondays or Fridays; that's when they're starting out the week's business or wrapping it up.

During the call, ask if they've submitted you for anything that week. Tell them any accomplishments or general submissions you made yourself. Only say positive things. Ask if they need you to drop off more headshots or demo reels.

Business gifts and lunches (tax-deductible, by the way) are a good opportunity to schmooze with the agent and make personal contact. Take yours to a brief lunch.

If they don't do this, bring coffee or doughnuts once every three months. Make your visit brief, very pleasant and totally professional. Find out your agent's birthday, always send a card and maybe even a small, business-like gift.

Listen to their advice. If they tell you to take new headshots, do it as quickly as possible. If they notice that you've gained weight and need to lose it—do it.

A good relationship is one thing. Sleeping with your agent is another. Don't. Or for that matter, don't house sit, watch the dogs, or wash the car. You're a client, not a slave.

Even with all this, you still might miss out on some auditions that would've been right for you. That's just the way it goes. When I was a working child actress, my agent—who had several child actresses with my look and age—submitted some of us for certain roles, and some of us for others.

Once, I remember auditioning for a guest star part on *The Brady Bunch* for the role of Greg's (Barry Williams) girlfriend.

At my callback, the producers (Sherwood Schwartz and Howard Leeds) offered me the part. I was ecstatic, but the next words from Howard were bittersweet: "Where were you when we were casting the regulars?"

Seems my agency didn't submit me for the part of Marcia, the oldest daughter, though others in my group were submitted. That's probably the first time, age 14, when I realized the harsh truth: Your agent, no matter how much they like you, doesn't submit you for every part you could play. Marcia, Marcia, Marcia!!

So agents make mistakes too. But always give them respect. They're human. Never forget it's a team effort, and never be bossy or sarcastic with them. Be firm and businesslike, but try not to argue.

But be willing to troubleshoot. Suppose you have an agent, you're doing the right things—but the agency still isn't submitting you.

Begin by keeping a diary: All the acting auditions you go on, the dates you gave headshots to the agent, the last time they called.

If your agent asked for 50 headshots in January, and now it's June, and they haven't asked you for any more headshots,

and you've not received any calls for auditions from them, something is very wrong. At least their Internet submissions of your photo to casting directors should have generated some auditions for you. The agency is obviously not focusing on promoting your career. It's time to set up an appointment to ask "Why?"—and if there's anything you can do to make it work.

If the agent keeps asking for headshots, and you're still not getting audition calls, it's one of three things.

YOU MAY NEED TO TAKE NEW PHOTOS, since the old ones apparently aren't the "magic picture" that gets you noticed.

IT'S THE TYPE OF ROLES your agent submits you for. Maybe the agent is crazy about you as a client, but sees you differently and is perhaps submitting you incorrectly.

THE OTHER POSSIBILITY, if all of the above is okay: Maybe your agent just doesn't have the juice to secure an audition for you.

If that's the case, ask yourself: Is it time to move on? Find different representation?

Before jumping in, first acknowledge that any change is stressful for human beings, whether it's moving to another town, getting a divorce, surviving the holidays—or leaving the agent you thought you'd be with forever. But sometimes, it's necessary.

If the problem can't be fixed, and if you haven't worked within 90 days, you may, according to SAG contract, write a letter to the agency and ask for your release from their representation. If you did not sign a SAG contract with your agent, you may not be able to cancel it that easily. But whatever your legal cancellation method is, be pleasant and firm with your letter. Make it brief, kind and simple. Leave out any lingering animosity or useless sarcasm. That's totally self-defeating behavior that could come back to haunt you.

MAKE SURE YOUR RELEASE LETTER IS KIND

If you are canceling a contract with a SAG agent, send your letter with a return receipt requested, send a copy to SAG, keep one for yourself, and start over.

Do you end your agreement before seeking new representation—or should you seek new representation before ending your old agreement? Every actor has an opinion on that. Just know that before signing with a new agent, you must send that letter to the old agent to disconnect.

Trends come and go regarding the way agents submit you for auditions. All headshot and resumé submissions was once by messenger service; by comparison, mail was too slow. Fax was never used, except in emergencies.

Today, most *commercial* submissions are done on the internet. Your agent posts your pictures on internet casting services, commercial casting directors check out these sites, and voila—they call to set up an audition.

That said, the majority of casting for *film and TV* is still done by messenger and the job breakdown services. Someday, these submissions will too be exclusively via the Internet.

MANAGERS

Now about managers. What are they and how are they different from an agent?

Back in the 60s, that was an easy question. A manager was someone you needed to guide your career, even if you were a good working actor with good agency representation.

Now a "manager" can be all kinds of things: Celebrity managers, aspiring-actor managers, and again, "F" type managers.

A reputable management services company can help an actor still looking for an agent. Remember the earlier example about the Venezuelan soap star; good managers can get you in to see agents for representation. And they often submit you for jobs (though they're really not supposed to do that).

Managers frequently charge more than agents, as much as 15 to 20% of your earnings. Some also charge an upfront fee. Some include photography service and acting lessons as well. They're also ungoverned by SAG rules, which is why there's plenty of bad out there mixed with the good.

So if you're considering a manager, ask for referrals. Talk to actors who've had a good experience with one. Check out every aspect of their service and ask questions. *And take your contract to an attorney, preferably one specializing in the entertainment field, before signing.* The manager's contract won't be a standard SAG contract, and you must make sure there's a way out if you're not satisfied with the service.

A word about agents and managers—they are like cats and dogs. The animosity is very near visceral; they have a natural disdain for each other. Still, many actors have both agents and managers and somehow manage to keep the uneasy alliance afloat. But never forget: Agents are mandatory. Managers are optional.

Maybe you'll get lucky. You could get an agent right at the start and grow old together. Or you may go through agents like Elizabeth Taylor goes through husbands. Here's hoping you have a smoother path than most actors have to travel.

BEFORE SIGNING WITH A MANAGER

- TAKE YOUR CONTRACT TO AN ENTERTAINMENT ATTORNEY FOR REVIEW.

- AND BE EQUALLY CAREFUL WITH THE ATTORNEY.

- ASK UP FRONT ABOUT THE FEE FOR REVIEWING THE CONTRACT.

STEP 6

YOUR UNION

The Product's Seal of Approval

The Screen Actors Guild is like the Supreme Court of the acting industry—an extension of the law.

It's a union that protects the actor, works hard to fight corruption, and keep things fair. Any union production made on film is covered by SAG, whether it's a movie, TV or commercial. (It's a union commercial if the advertising company is a SAG signatory. If not, don't plan on making residuals—monies you're paid each time your commercial is shown.)

Another union—AFTRA, the American Federation of Television and Radio Artists—covers any union production on videotape or radio.

Any production not registered with SAG or AFTRA is non-union.

Basically, this means the production can pay the actor anything, or for that matter, nothing. There's nobody looking over the production to make sure the actor is treated fairly.

In your industry, the Screen Actors Guild is the law

The unions decide an actor's base pay rate, ensure the production pays the actor in full, and keeps close watch on residuals. Both unions have excellent health insurance coverage, credit unions offering loan and bank services for members, free or reduced-price screenings of current movies and a legal department if you're treated unfairly or sexually harassed by a producer.

Non-union actors don't have any of this. Union actors do. How do you join?

The fees and the how-to change over the years, so check with your local SAG or AFTRA branch for updates. That said, here are the basics:

AFTRA

To join AFTRA, you pay a one-time registration fee and you're in. Right now, it's about one thousand dollars.

From then on, you only pay a yearly fee, very small and adjusted according to your earnings as an actor. After joining, you can obtain a list of all casting directors who handle videotape programs (soap operas and some reality and children's TV, for instance).

SAG

Joining SAG is a little more complicated.

You pay your one-time registration fee—like AFTRA, it's well over a thousand dollars. But you can't join until meeting the ever-changing prerequisites. Again, check with your local union branch for updates.

Another way to be eligible: the Taft-Hartley way, as described earlier. This happens mostly through commercials, but it's also possible with appearances on TV and movies. If we want you in our project badly enough, we will take a non-union actor, employ you in our project and "Taft-Hartley" you, which is the legal term for making you eligible to be a union member. It's easier to do this for commercials. For movies and television, the production company usually has to pay a large fine to the union.

Another way into SAG is simply to join AFTRA for one year, get one AFTRA voucher for work, and at the end of the year be SAG eligible. Once again, check with union officials for current rules, fees and membership requirements.

The unions cover not only principle actors, but background players as well.

AEA

For those primarily interested in theater, there is a union called Actor's Equity Association (AEA). Equity will provide the actor with all of the same great protection and pay scales for theatre performances. Check with your local Equity union branch for current fees and prerequisites for joining.

AGVA

Another union which covers live performances for entertainers is AGVA, the American Guild of Variety Artists. This is not really the concern of actors.

My advice: Do what it takes to become a *union* actor.

STEP 7

YOUR NETWORKING

Promoting the Product

Incredibly, this is the step most often ignored by an aspiring actor. But without it, your career can come to a dead halt—even with a strong product such as yourself, armed with a great look, good acting skills, a hard-working agent, eye-catching headshots, an ever-expanding resumé and a union card.

Plan to network for your entire career. Here's what you shouldn't do:

Never sit at home waiting for the phone to ring. Never say, "My agent doesn't call me enough," or "I don't go out on enough auditions," or "Maybe it's just slow." Fact is, it's never really slow. There's always enough going on for a clever and pro-active actor to find work. Here are some suggestions:

Don't forget to work your agent. That's in Step 5.

Learn what's going on in the industry. Do this by *reading the trades*.

My favorite here on the West Coast is *The Hollywood Reporter*. It tells you about movies and TV programs in production, pre- and post-. It tells you "who's who" in the industry. It familiarizes you with names of studios and production companies. It gives you a feel for the business.

Also check out, particularly at the start of your career: *Back Stage West* (on the West Coast) and *Back Stage East* on the East Coast. They keep you current on TV and movie trends, current top-selling genres and the type of look that's hot right now.

And of course, there's always *Variety*—

the weekly version (a daily in Los Angeles and New York).

But don't just passively read the trades. Instead, as you review them, look for the names of casting directors, agents, producers and directors. Keep a file on each industry professional. Keep a running record of the projects they've been involved in. Also, you may obtain the names from the credits on the shows that you watch. Also keep a record of every industry professional you audition for, or meet, and the results of each meeting.

Then as you prepare to audition for someone, pull out that person's file and see precisely what they've cast, produced or directed. Knowing more about them may give you a leg up. It will certainly help you feel more comfortable about meeting them.

ANOTHER WAY TO NETWORK:

CONTRIBUTE TIME OR MONEY TO A CHARITY THAT INVOLVES CELEBRITIES, PRODUCERS AND DIRECTORS.

True, annual fundraising dinners are expensive, but you're contributing to a great cause, you get a tax deduction, and you might rub elbows with Steven Spielberg. And if that happens—if you're at one of these events and find yourself next to the head of an agency or a famous director—remember the Bible: "Ask and you shall receive."

Tell your new friend that you're an actor and would like to audition for future jobs. Hand out a business card with your photo and agency contact number on it. Simple as that.

It's also not a bad idea to hang at restaurants frequented by celebrities. Stop in for tea or salad and you might run into someone who can help you. Try places near the studios. Plenty of industry people go there every day.

Do blind mailouts. Purchase an updated directory for casting directors (they're available at Samuel French Bookstores on the West Coast and The Drama Book Shop on the East Coast). Check out the production offices listed in the trades, then send a brief cover letter, photo and resumé to them as a general submission, requesting consideration for "any part that would apply."

There are websites that post current casting notices that are available for actors to use to submit themselves for new jobs. But a word of caution: Be careful when submitting to these services, and never go to anyone's home or a strange, isolated place to audition.

Some actors are also writers: A commercial script is often a vehicle to carry them into working actor status. Look at Sylvester Stallone and *Rocky*. Or Matt Damon and Ben Affleck with *Good Will Hunting*. Or Chuck Norris.

Every casting director you meet is an opportunity to audition for more roles. Win one over, and they'll call you for other parts, even if you don't make it on the first try.

Commercials you are in are also a commercial on "you" as an actor, and everybody sees them!

David Leisure is a great example. He was a character actor who won the part of Joe Isuzu for the now-famous car commercials. He was so good as a comedic character in that first commercial—as well as being pleasant and professional—that Isuzu hired him to do an entire campaign for them. Then he got a regular co-starring role on *Empty Nest*, playing the same comedic character.

Along with his talent, it was all about David's networking—from one audition to one commercial to a series of commercials—to a TV series.

Lucille Ball, a successful actor in B-movies before making it in *I Love Lucy*, used to say that every job always led to another. Each part you get can help you get more parts.

YOU MAY ASK:

ONCE I GET A REGULAR GIG
EITHER IN MOVIES, TV OR COMMERCIALS
CAN I EASE UP ON MY NETWORKING?

7

ANSWER: ARE YOU KIDDING?

Once you land a starring or co-starring part in a movie or TV series, use that to make sure producers, directors and casting agents notice you.

First phase: Send them post cards (with your picture on the front).

Second: Place an ad in the major trade papers. This is called a "tune-in" ad.

Then: Hire a publicist. Advertise yourself as an actor.

Most important of all: Never burn bridges. Be a positive

and professional delight. Never carry personal problems or an attitude into the workplace. Start building a good reputation right now. Be a clean-living and positive role model for all the young people who will be your fans.

At this point, you may be at the end of the book—but you're at the beginning of your journey.

So keep the book and the accompanying DVD with you along the way. Consult them frequently. The more you read it—or view it—the more insight you'll gain into the acting business.

May you have much success in your career—and fun along the way! God bless you!

GLOSSARY

ACROSS THE BOARD: When an agent represents an actor in all areas of performance.

BUMP: The additional compensation extras receive for doing special business in a scene or for use of their car, props, etc.

CALLBACK: You've done such a great job on an interview, they're calling you and some other actors back to meet with either the producer, director or advertiser to decide if you would be right for the project.

CALL TIME: The time actors are due on the set.

CAMERA RIGHT/LEFT: The direction of which way to move when facing the camera.

CLAPBOARD: That famous piece of equipment that is clapped down at the start of a scene. It indicates the name of the director, the scene number and other critical information. It is used immediately when sound and cameras start rolling.

CLOSE SHOT: A close-up of a person or object in front of the camera.

COLD READING: An audition where you are asked to read lines without rehearsal—or just after a quick glance.

COMMERCIAL AGENCY REPRESENTATION: When an agent represents an actor solely for commercials.